HOODLUM BIRDS

HOODLUM BIRDS

EUGENE GLORIA

PENGUIN POETS

PENGUIN BOOKS

Published by the Penguin Group

Penguin Group (USA) Inc., 375 Hudson Street, New York, New York 10014, U.S.A.

Penguin Group (Canada), 90 Eglinton Avenue East, Suite 700, Toronto, Ontario, Canada M4P 2Y3 (a division of Pearson Penguin Canada Inc.)

Penguin Books Ltd, 80 Strand, London WC2R 0RL, England

Penguin Ireland, 25 St Stephen's Green, Dublin 2, Ireland (a division of Penguin Books Ltd)

Penguin Group (Australia), 250 Camberwell Road, Camberwell, Victoria 3124, Australia (a division of Pearson Australia Group Pty Ltd)

Penguin Books India Pvt Ltd, 11 Community Centre, Panchsheel Park, New Delhi – 110 017, India

Penguin Group (NZ), cnr Airborne and Rosedale Roads, Albany, Auckland 1310, New Zealand (a division of Pearson New Zealand Ltd)

Penguin Books (South Africa) (Pty) Ltd, 24 Sturdee Avenue, Rosebank, Johannesburg 2196, South Africa

Penguin Books Ltd, Registered Offices:
80 Strand, London WC2R 0RL, England

First published in the United States of America by Penguin Books 2006

10 9 8 7 6 5 4 3 2 1

LIBRARY OF CONGRESS CATALOGING-IN-PUBLICATION DATA
Gloria, Eugene.
  Hoodlum Birds / Eugene Gloria.
     p. cm.
  ISBN 0-14-303644-0
     I. Title.
PS3557.L6485H66 2006
811'.54—dc22   2005052125

Printed in the United States of America
Designed by Sabrina Bowers

For Karen

Anxious or secure, my soul is yours

CONTENTS

PART 3

PART 4

Look, broken-winged, the bird
You own has come back home.

— MAHSATI

AFTERWARDS

Swirls and numerals craze the sky,
        A misplaced sun and cardinals
                On the black, perfunctory branches,

Slate of cursives and Chinese calligraphy.
        Who will bear witness to these hands?

Look at this traveling light,
        An incandescent bubble bouncing like an apple
                Fallen off a branch. In China,

The Bo people carved trees into coffins
        And buried their dead in the highest cliffs.
                No one yet knows why they did this.

There is sun everywhere: on my sleeve,
        On my hair, a long falling strand. I am
                Scrolling up and down the diminutive print

For names I grew up with like Agbayani,
        Estrella, Pinaroc, Santos. I grow distant and vague.
                We leave and return with empty pockets. We live

In towns of conveniences and complacencies.
        If you are reading this, I am nobody to you,

Except for this loneliness we keep
        And this heart, and you listening.

1

PART 1

THE LAW

Ávila, 1982

When the civil guards approached me
and asked me for my papers,

I pictured the face of a sunny saint
being disemboweled on the rack.

Widows in perennial black, addicts of prayer,
find comfort here the way monks

in hair shirts must take to penance,
or me, addled in my blissed-out days

in San Francisco, tugging daily on a roach.
And that's how I must've been,

befogged in Ávila on a visit
that coincided with the papal tour.

A murder of crows, clerics, nuns in wimples,
tarring the field with their black habits.

St. Francis de Sales dispenses, "The measure
of love is to love without measure."

This republic of goodness
was once peopled with spies. Maybe

that's what got the saints in trouble,
their willingness to surrender

once found out. I know authority
when I see it make a U-turn to pull me over.

I also know that the Burgos Christ
in pageant-red skirt is tethered to a story,

its weals and welts, blue-black,
the wounds Nicodemus witnessed as he

lowered Jesus, alone in his discarded body.
The carving by Nicodemus

would one day float its way
first to a monastery, then to Burgos.

When the civil guards approached me
and asked me for my papers,

I felt for a string around my neck, my scapular
like a leaf pressed on the road of pistils and stamens.

That moment stood
for something I can no longer recall.

What with those men and their gift
of whiteness, their constant need of proof.

I must've smiled at them, clueless yet longing
to be profound.

SONG IN THE FORM OF A WHITE SUIT

By night on my bed I sought him, the schoolteacher in a suit,
White as the moon dancing in the square.

By night, the civil guards have gone to their loved ones,
Their wives with fat hands and children

Sallow with affection for the air they breathe.
I could write their entire lives on a napkin.

When the schoolteacher asked them to define the soul,
The children groused at his question, thinking it another trick

Made up by grown-ups with questionable ancestors.
By night in my bed I called out to the one I love,

Knowing that he would be gone. How fair is it to want
When to love the crisp syllables of red wine

From the river Oja, or the mountains of camphor,
Is easier than breathing the spice of his skin.

I want the white linens of his bed, this *contest of flowers,*
This transient joy, his hair in my lips, my breasts

Feeding among the white lilies of the schoolteacher's hands.
I will go to the square where the empty benches

Have turned their full attention to the moon.
By night I will seek out his white face,

The one I love, *floating, floating like a gourd,*
Floating along the river Oja.

ARDOR

When he found his faith,

He tossed his armor, sword, and citizenship.
It must have been quite a spectacle

To see Sebastian return to his pockmarked handlers,
Former associates in the elite Praetorian Guards,

His five wounds not yet healed,
To proclaim love for his Pure Commander.

Goodness, in all its dark depravity,
Takes a woman in love:

Blindfolds her, then when she's aroused,
Pulls out his cock to piss on her.

As in the "Song of Songs," the sweet perfume
Of the bridegroom lures the bride's attendants,

So the scent of martyrs, the dew-dropped
Rhododendrons, the spread-eagled roses of abbeys,

Must arouse enough goodness in us.
When I look beyond the burnished fields of oats,

The sunflowers shoulder high,
The mute purples of ground clovers, I recall

This smell that made me think of St. Sebastian.
In Rome, I mistook it for my waiter's sweat,

The leaves of the balsam poplar
Upwind from the sidewalk café.

Here in Lavigny, it is the rain-washed daffodils
In this open field, a saint's odor of sanctity.

OBEDIENCE

Agustín fills up the yellow wheelbarrow
                with fallen nuts from almond trees
across the road from Beatriz Beckett's horse.

                Kicking up dirt, the mare bobs
    and shakes her mane black as fresh asphalt.
                She stomps in long muscled strides

on the hottest day in Andalucía.
                I wear all black like the moon that plays
a speaking part in the drama set in Nijar.

In the story, the groom named Casimero
                labors in the fields, then takes his siesta
as on any ordinary day.
                He is his mother's only son.

In the newspaper account,
the bride has a limp and crossed eyes—
                but the details here are unimportant,

since the moon in the play has a speaking part.
                Maybe the moon lacks mercy, the way the sun
anneals a man who wears all black?

                Francesca, the bride (yes, she had a name)
might as well have been a dead flower
                on her brother's wide lapel.

If there is any sense to be gotten
			from what the moon had to say,
desire would have nothing of it.

In Lorca's play,
the nameless bride describes Leonardo
			as a raging river and her groom as a spot of water.

In Carlos Saura's film, you have to imagine
			a horse conveying Leonardo and the runaway bride.
In hand claps and guitars,
			two knives
sway like the sword inside the matador's cape,
			then blood flows in silken scarves.

Tonight I frame a tiny planet
			from my dormer window.

The petal of an iris turns
			a backward glance at the moon.
Obedience is Agustín's slow but even gait
			as he makes his way toward
Beatriz Beckett's horse
			to groom her and tend to her needs.

GOODNESS

I couldn't contain my hands
from touching the blue and yellow
tiles, the chiseled flourish
of flowers and poems in Arabic
on window frames and doorways
more solemn than a congress of saints.
Such goodness strikes me like panic,
or like the aching beauty
of harelip petals of dogwood blooms.

I remember the two of us young in our bones,
when goodness taught us to sleep side by side,
her waist against mine,
all sea and brine tangled in her hair.

What is it in beauty that renders us helpless?
Awful goodness is what the saints must suffer,
unlike the pleasure we know
when the store clerk gives us change
for a twenty when we handed him only a ten.
Today while folding my shirts and socks
and placing them in cedar drawers
I was suffused with this spell
of goodness as if desire
planted its fist in my solar plexus.

My sister looked after me the way
a lighthouse draws ships to safer harbors.
Faultless as a daylily, a lightness
in her step as if God, who seldom chose unwisely,

had plucked her
roots and petals from His garden.

Last we spoke, my sister,
now some corporate fiscal boss,
was learning me to be
money-wise—sound advice
on aggressive growth mutual funds.
She's mastered the language of deep pockets,
endowments, and the prospect of daily gain.
Money is to her the only measure.

Liquid assets, fat cats in jaunty ascots,
and all the future's other aliases
are nothing more than this bloated present,
of which beauty has no part.
What moved in the dim corridors
I can only say was the spirit of God.
And from there I returned to discover
my waning eyesight,
to squint and filter in the light
of my dislocated origins.

Before desire, goodness was nothing
to Adam and Eve. There were
only the chores in the garden
and God's watchful eye.
And that was it. Nothing.
Goodness calling upon their duties,
their previous lives of nothingness.

BOABDIL'S EVICTION

All his life he struggled at how to ask,
unable to talk to his father.
Instead of the right questions, he learns to mimic

the musings of women.
How else does one assume a nonsalaried office?
Every room and every portal framing an open window,

in a house full of answers,
become creeds, fragments of truth,
songs chiseled in tile. A mother's ambition

turns into the rented air he breathes.
So when the new tenants arrived
with their trailers of ostentatious furniture,

he barely had time to pack.
Far enough on the back roads where his neighbors
could not see his abrupt departure, he turns around to see,

first his home and then his orange trees.
God, whose penchant for punishment is legend,
would have been kinder to zap him into stone.

But here, the ill-starred and the ordinary have more
in common with the likes of him; hitched
on the muzzy edges: a footnote, a sigh.

MOJÁCAR

At ten in Spain, the night is just beginning. Dogs barking,
Birds brawling, meals being set.

"Walt Disney was conceived in this house,"
Charo, my host, tells me. His mother a maid,

His father a prominent physician. This is a deniable fact.
In my dream, I look down from my balcony

At the plaza below. A horse-drawn cortege waits.
Nuns in black habits

Convene like crows feeding on stones.
Birds in the bougainvillea vines legislate and filibuster.

I am my brilliant colonizer, languishing
Over a modest meal. Marissa, the barmaid, serves up

Wedges of cantaloupe with thin slices of ham, roast pork
Cooked with rosemary and pine nuts, fried potatoes,

Chicken adobo, and a small bottle of rioja. Charo at the Torreón
Is telling me a story in a language I almost understand.

I can smell the heat blowing through the window.
Embers of furnace, dust of my forefathers,

An excavation
Sifting ceramics and bones.

No more *jamón serrano*, I say, just chamomile tea.
Two spoons of elm powder with water to cure my nausea.

My mother would say drink 7UP three times a day.
Say, boil water with salt and sugar for diarrhea.

My eyeballs are fried, I think, from the dust and heat.
A pharmacist says infection from dirty towels.

I'm not American here: dark and foreign—Asian at best.
Clear voices breeze through the bougainvillea.

Inside a white *arrabal,* a shirtless man with long pants.
"You do well to weep as a woman."

I fast and purge, the *servicio* steps away from the balcony.
My wife left me to return to America.

Once in a garden concert, petals of jasmine fell on my lap.
Remember the hyacinths of Sevilla, the oranges of Andalucía?

My wife writes in her gorgeous cursive.
The *E* and the *u* of my name are like petals of bougainvillea.

BILBAO, SPAIN

It will always be afternoon, the cello groans.
        Hands unbuttoning a blue blouse:
the afternoon of the tourist in need of a nap,

        the minutes the desk clerk devotes to daydream,
the streetlight's emptying hours of directives.

What sounds like lament
            seeps through the walls like the Sea Hag's
flute from the island of Goons.

            No, it isn't like torment
        Nor can it matter if we swear to change our lives.
It isn't like birdcalls from a covey

nor church bells from the square.
            It lacks the urgency of mama's voice
        when she forgets about her birds.

At first, we thought it too loud and intrusive,
            then it drenched us the way fog

splashes like water over the distant hills,
            and the player practicing was disciplined—
        her cello suite was Bach's.

The days we were billeted there,
            she would begin precisely at two
        then quit at four. I'd sleep right through,

then waken shortly. My wife nursing a cold
                would sleep some more, and me, I'd pause

to record the food we ate, what we purchased,
                and where we'd sleep the next night.

I want nothing else, only a hand,
a wounded hand, if possible.

—FEDERICO GARCÍA LORCA

THE FACTORY

The smell of burnt log
       mixes with the trapped-in cold.

What's in here will stay.
       Much like an apothecary's shop

with blue decanters labeled
       witch hazel, eucalyptus, lilac,

this room is bottled winter. Scent
       of cold, scent of warped wax and wood.

I am inside my grandfather's room:
       driftwood and stone.

He is cutting paper into triangles,
       folding them into tiny boxes

he will stuff with petals
       of tuberoses and frangipani,

his remedy for homesickness.
       I am in my studio and a bee-loud

intruder signals his anxiety,
       his need for departure.

You could say he's dilatory in his habits,
       in abeyance from his factory tasks.

I know better than he does
        about the glass window. I know

that he will not get through.
        But certain scents—the lilacs in spring,

the star magnolias round as dinner plates
        blossoming near the Puritan graveyard,

act as a stay against what awaits us.
        I recall my grandfather's funeral

and the feast his third wife prepared.
        Delinquent fathers and unpunctual

uncles, wives, and sisters-in-law
        gathered round a coffin curved like a boat.

Boats like coffins drift in the sea.
        I take a drinking glass and coaster

and snare the bee inside,
        think of the Jains who pour

sugared water on the asphalt
        to feed the ants. I let the insect go.

Back to his presses and widgets,
back to his factory of flowers.

PART 2

ECONOMY

With their bedsheets on the sidewalk,
the immigrant vendors hawk a stream of scarves
in waves of colors more floral than a field of lavender.

On the first day of my pilgrimage,
my feet insisted the permanence of dirt.
The road we loved will not remember us.

That day I walked four leagues,
a thousand aches pierced my body,
then I came to a pass with a line of apple blossoms.

Nights I ventured into the comfort
of tablecloths, silverware, and china, meals
that arrived in courses.

A solitary bird surrounded by tables
with couples cooing at each other.
Then another day

and another would pass
until I began to consider the stone
I harbored in my shoe.

I shook it out and said, "Stone,
I canonize thee into sainthood."
My patron of blisters knew exactly what to do

on the surface of a lake. And water, too,
I blessed. Its sweetness beneath the beating
rays of sun, and for miles and miles, water

sistered the stone in silence. In my sickness,
I took to prayers, turned to the hour's lonely keep
when words I mumbled became my only wages.

Weeks later, I see them,
the immigrant vendors: scarves in rows
on dingy bedsheets.

Their faces oily and dark—
some might even say they look like me.
Just when their risky commerce begins to pay off,

the law arrives with vengeance and, swift
as thieves, they swoop up their loot, their ventures
collapsing like circus tents.

FEMALE FIGURE (SIBYL WITH ERASURE)

A plant with pink petals in blossom time
        insists a presence from the cracks of a ruin.
                Such defiance I cannot claim

in the way I sign my name on the ledger at the hotel.
        My mark infers an absence,
                its swift flowing gesture illegible.

And even here, sitting with my café solo
        behind a wall of glass,
                I could be invisible to the schoolboys

clawing at the glass
        for someone's attention.
                I remember a time in Manila when I could disappear

into a crowd, the street swallowing me whole
        in the blue light, and then emerge wholly myself
                like a compound sentence memorized

from a grammar book. I was free
        to open my mouth and babble
                the basic nouns and verbs of children. It was in

December when my colleagues took me out
        for a drink at a nightclub in Quezon City. A woman
                on the spotlighted stage stood in a state of undress,

unclasping her bra,
        tired music accompanied the watery
                motions of her arms and hips.

As her hands slurred south to her waist,
      a man rushed the stage with his jacket
            covering the dancer as a fireman blankets a fire victim.

Then the lights came on, a brief commotion
      seized all conversation.
            My colleague who taught fiction and drama

stamped his cigarette out on the ashtray and said,
      "Christmas money. Even cops need
            to shop for Christmas." It was a shakedown.

Then the music came back, I think it was 4 Non Blondes.
      We finished our drinks and left. It is almost two o'clock,
            the streets here in Santiago are nearly empty,

shops lock their doors, closed for the afternoon.
      Workers pull out keys to enter their apartments,
            fresh bread protruding from paper sacks.

In this rare sunlight, the pink blossoms
      expose their modesty, exempt from history.

THE VERB *TO LICK*

The woman employed by the tourist council hates her job.
She's the last in a series of guides I've met

with a new version of San Roque's legend.
What's common coin relates a story of a wound

on the leg of this pilgrim with a dog,
sometimes holding a roll of bread in its mouth.

In Santiago, you always see vagabonds with dogs.
One sad mutt so beat it tried to lay its head

on the satchel of its master panhandling in the street.
Pity comes more easily to the animal, which demands

pathos in our lives. This mutt coiled in the rain.
I bent down to stroke his chummy head,

my hand telling him that I sleep in a warm house.
But when he saw my walking stick, he cowered.

Cruelty made the guide who hates her job
examine the dog and the pilgrim saint's wound.

Cruel because swinging from one language to another
is done on a greased pole,

and cruel because I wanted to hear her mouth
the sensual with her poor English.

Her Spanish sounds like sunlight drying a wet shirt.
And in the process, I've grown fond of her.

She's *delicadeza*, a word that names her nature.
Whose dream deepens in the rain? Whose hair is lilacs?

Her mind hums and searches until a petal of tongue appears.
A teacher once advised us that if a poem is going nowhere,

then make someone lick or suck something.
And so I made her do it.

Her tongue exposed
is what the dog does to San Roque's wound.

The rain in Galicia is a kind of thinking,
wet stones prefacing a patina of rust.

The dog that nurtures the saint with bread is nothing.
It is cruelty that satisfies the flesh.

MARTYRDOM OF ST. EULALIA

One soldier is short
and has to climb a ladder.

The other soldier is tall enough
to work on her right hand
with just his upraised arms.

Her cross is a giant *X,* no headrest,
no insignia in Latin.

Think of the implication of the *X.*
This spacey teen gibbeted

in our town square like the blue light
special in the center aisle. Her legs,
therefore, are spread-eagled.

Her breasts are bared,
but her waist is loosely wrapped
by a hint of cloth. The soldier atop
the ladder is staring at her face,

not at the knot he's tightening on her wrist.
He can barely smell her fear.

The soldier in near fetal pose below the cross
is a phrase contained
within Eulalia's legs. He is her agonizing brother.

His body averted,
arms shielding his face in shame.

His sword's handle protrudes
behind his back like an awkward erection,
its helmeted tip points north, northeast.

This bas-relief is marble white
like the Stations of the Cross
above long cathedral columns.

There are seven men in all. Three
soldiers suggest a ménage à trois
framing the crucifixion.

Another three are standing by,
but look away. All are captured
in pixel time. I am in the far left corner,

silhouetted in the margins.
As night grows, I hear
sporadic laughter, smell the girl's singed hair.

HOODLUM BIRDS

The fearless blackbirds see me again
at the footpath beside the tall grasses
sprouting like unruly morning hair.
They caw and caw like vulgar boys
on street corners making love to girls
with their "hey mama
this" and their "hey mama that."
But this gang of birds is much too slick.
They are my homeys of the air
with their mousse-backed hair and Crayola
black coats like small fry hoods who smoke
and joke about each other's mothers,
virginal sisters, and the sweet arc of revenge.
These birds spurn my uneaten celery sticks,
feckless gestures, ineffective hosannas.
They tag one another, shrill and terrible,
caroling each to each my weekly wages.
But they let me pass, then flit away.
They won't mess with me this time—
they know where I live.

EL AVE CHRISTINA

Everyone fled from the church but me
when pale Christina cartwheeled from her coffin
and, like a house martin, flitted up
the beams and perched there for a while.
It took some doing from the priest
and me to coax her down finally.
From cataleptic fits to dresses in rags,
this kook, this meshuggeneh,
has been called everything but holy.
In her sleep of death she saw

the priest, his mistress,
the butcher with the baker's wife,
our chaste aunts in their masculine suits,
and ash-gray purgatorial pants.
Her hoot-owl eyes would never lie;
the disquieting lurch, the birdlike way
she nibbles her bread, are not fabrics
of an overwrought head. She'd jump
into the river with its fresh sheet of snow,
crawl into the clay oven with the blaze
licking at her sparrow's breast,
and sky up the treetop branches
to flee from the stink of our flesh.

When our parish priest mumbled:
"We entreat into thy hands, most merciful Father,
The soul of this our child departed—"
and my sister shot up like embers to the rafters,
the distant God of orphans

must have made her choose
between the scented angels
singing or this stench of sister skin.
Were it not for me she wouldn't be here.
Even the God of Job must have heard
the prayers of the pure and simple,
and no doubt, my sister's, too.
In middle life, as if reborn into another,
she's learned to live among the likes of us,
the unholy and the great unwashed, while
chastising counts and up-and-coming saints.

SLEEPING WITH *BUTLER'S LIVES OF THE SAINTS*

After Octavio Paz

What's most human must drive
an arrow to the heart.

Ghosts, too, must abide by this directive
& remain transparent,

going about their business in old houses.
Before I was an *I,* I longed to be ethereal.

Sprouting wings at will & gliding through
cul-de-sacs and malls around the valley.

My hands, too, would gradually disappear
followed by my arms, then neck & head

until my whole body was slight as allergen.
Before I was an *I,* I spoke an old language

that would return on drowsy afternoons.
Therefore I struggled to say

the simplest sentences. So much so
that the maligned semicolon

became an ardent ally, an island
of pause and the deep breath.

The comma, too, bless its tiny soul,
was the crumb which the god

of small favors multiplied
tenfold for my morning pie.

Before I was an *I,* knowledge
clung to me like burrs & hunger

guided my ship like *the barefoot light
on the sleeping land & sea.*

Go get some water,
And wash this filthy witness from your hand.

—LADY MACBETH

MOTET

The husband hears *lagrima y fortuna*
        from the fortune-teller reading his palm.

Having asked the wrong questions,
        his sentence is to live here the rest of his life.

The wife nurses a nosebleed.
        She's a tall drink of water.

The wife kisses his neck,
        blood petals on his collar.

Nowhere else can a man imagine the rain
        in his hands, or conspire on white sheets

with the rain whispering
        sweet talk in Spanish.

Boarding the next bus,
        one foot on the sidewalk,

the husband mistakes happiness
        for a loosened apron, a pear

ripening on the sill,
        his wife's hair tucked behind an ear.

PART 3

AUBADE

Because grief straggles like a bottom dweller
And seldom comes up for air,
He slides one hand through a jacket sleeve

And slings pole and fishing gear in his trunk.
Grief is a basement thing—
A bad mix like drinking and driving if

One is young and openhearted. He drives
His car to the Sacramento Delta. The air
Frigid, the odor of human salt reeks

From his chest. His hands so cold
They could barely hook the worm at the end
Of his line. He lions in the morning,

Sucking breath into breath with his last pack
Of smokes. The inland heat still asleep
In the ground. Nothing but a low moan,

A humming song rises up from a well
Inside his wasted self.
It had no lyrics, this chorus about waiting

In Puccini's opera where a woman full of hope
Peers through a hole pinprick size
To see the harbor lights drag in

The ship that would bring home her beloved.
There are no words for the sun's arrival
Except that it is begotten by song,

A fire spark flickering Pentecostal,
A nascent thing, immigrant and lonely.
Morning begets the honking of geese

The way birds and light beget his happiness
For a father, whom he recalls impeccably
Dressed for his daily departure,

And how the father would pause to hum
His affections, and bless him
With the bread from the oven of his heart.

TWO BLONDES AND A TURQUOISE CADILLAC

A man driving a turquoise Cadillac
would not know the nothing that happens

in poetry as he cruises
his Caddy through a fog in central Oregon.

The two blondes beside him, K & S—
more contraband than cargo to *Mister Charlie,*

more cargo than intimates
who bared their breasts at a secluded hot springs

in the heart of redneck country.
Long tall conifers,

peeled jeans steaming on rocks,
pink nipples, swirl of snow, water

bubbling from the roiling gut of earth,
and happiness descending

like petals from the cataract-gray sky.
They were students who knew grief only as students,

understood love as a landslide just waiting to happen.
It was then that his girlfriend, K, fell in love

with S, and S began contemplating
a career in fastpitch softball.

That day the turquoise Cadillac
maneuvered through the thick valley fog.

Imagine them as salmon on the run,
inside the murk and hurry to spawn upstream,

think of the car containing them
as the self surging forward

as if to fill a void, think of the void
as history they will one day retrieve.

ALLEGRA WITH SPIRIT

Even the dead is cold in 1967,
        the dead shivering in his trousers.
Allegra waits for the bus
        on Union and Van Ness,
            her arms wide around a paper sack.
A car stopped at the light is playing Rodrigo.

The melody is red, the Spanish earth,
        all manner of color thrown from the car window.
Allegra wouldn't know Rodrigo from Elgar,
        Elgar from Miles, only that the 47
isn't running on time
        on still-wet streets from a spell of rain.

Here, then, is winter in 1967
        when the dead has come to visit
            inside an insomniac's dream. The dead
shivering in his trousers, betraying a promise
        by crossing the water on a secret boat
just to tell her he is hungry. In the long ago,
        she whispered in his good ear
when he was very sick; and she, his girl
        spooning him the bitter medicine, begged
him never to visit when he is dead.
        In 1967, when eucalyptus leaves could cleanse
the air's palate with their antiseptic blue,
        a bus, as if from some great vanishment on roads
that climb and bend but never want to end,
        a white and mock orange bus emerges
like a tardy backdoor man, a pallid innuendo.

A woman waiting for the bus has staked her faith
              in the hour's luck, in the bony air
of the alley she wades through to get to the street
              that is dark as a paper sack.
There is only the rice she washes daily
              and what she carries in the paper sack: eggs, bread,
                    salt for memory, a can of milk, fish
for the tamarind soup
                    she'll pray over with the rice.
Allegra would like to tell the dead to go
              because there is nothing here to take back.
In his secret boat, the dead carries
              his bowl of air and shivers in his trousers.

BEAUTY

She has an axe to grind with our lizard-eyed neighbors,
says they called her a bitch, her mother one, too,
all because she wears her skirt short,
and those high-heeled sandals make her hips sway.
But that doesn't give them the right, she'd say.
Yelling from one end of the street
to the other lizard mothers and lizard maids.
And once she grabbed one maid by the ponytail
and dragged her down to the ground like a mop.
The two girls had tears on their faces,
my sister's smeared with mascara.

Her final stint in formal instructions was marred
by her run-in with Sister Mary George:
the usual thing, her plaid skirt was hiked up too high
and her eyes overpainted.
"What reputation do you want our school to have?"
Sister Mary George's eyes sharpened to a slit.
On Yom Kippur she came to class
with a Star of David stenciled on one cheek.
A week after, she was expelled; stories
about my sister regaled our dinner table.
Her strangeness traced far back
to when we spoke a different language,
when she was banished to Misericordia
in Manila where our mother's mother lived.
Life with Lola was Papillon in the French Guyana.
Our lola was more austere than devout,
harsh with chores and prone to cuss.

Like the rest of us at the table, my sister sat rapt
as if hearing for the first time someone else's story.

But my favorite is the one about her fall.
The one, my mother says, that explains her nature.
It was around the time Errol Flynn
played Robin Hood at the Ever Theater.
My brother Boy with his bamboo stick
for a sword and his green vest and green shorts
was playing Robin Hood with my sister.
He was evading imaginary foes and flew
up to the two-story window ledge.
When he slipped, my sister leapt after him
as if her hand could pull him up.
And more than my brother, she had
her brains scrambled from the fall,
or so we're told.
              In our family lore,
she is three bricks shy of a full load.
One sandwich short of a picnic.
But in the story she tells her son,
she was the pretty one who often
got in trouble, but always managed.
She is the one I think of now
as my Air France stewardess pops
a can of tonic water, lime, and a splash
of vodka, and her white teeth,
in little rows, could undo
even the sharpest one among us.

RENO

The Greyhound bus had shuttled him back
and forth with forty, sixty bucks in his pocket,

chump change parlayed in slots and blackjack tables,
then the five-hour drive back

barely enough to catch up on sleep.
Mr. Santos was a dapper old-timer

with his felt fedora, Pendleton shirt
buttoned at the collar, and herringbone coat.

He smoked fat cigars, regaled us with stories
of trapping pigeons on park benches

with his hat then cooking them for dinner.
I was his baby Buddha with a round belly

on which he rubbed his hands for luck,
before shooing me away with a silver dollar.

My father could not separate him from my uncle
who loved the ponies.

My uncle who excelled in law school,
but checked out by clacking mahjong tiles

from dusk until the jeepneys started
trolling the streets for fares in early light.

In Montague, where a sign reads, SLOW CHILDREN PLAYING,
where in an old mill converted into a bookstore,

I found a book of poems, art, stories,
a black-and-white photo, a composition of gray,

and lit faces linked in some universal feeling,
an oblique flag draped over Mr. Santos's open casket.

And suddenly I'm set apart from this aisle of books
the way a pencil draws a line on the page

between viewer and image where in the center
a man is reduced to his dimensions,

and I'm shuttling back to what I was when I knew him
coming home from his trip to Reno,

his balding head pressed against the Greyhound bus window,
a lucky man with his winnings fat in his pocket.

THESE HANDS

Long ago, he wore gloves to drive his car
because his hands would slide on the steering wheel.

His tentative foot on the gas pedal,
causing that carsick heave of his Fairlane 500.

Today I motor the wind and loop
of Skyline Boulevard, the stitch and pull

of the seamstress sewing the zigzag ride.
My hands on the wheel become my father's.

Once my father fell asleep at the wheel
and woke on the soft shoulder of the road,

unhurt but so unnerved that he never drove
at night again. These hands drive

along the dreaming pages of my journal,
a dreaming that drove my father

to the margins of the white-lined causeway.
When the Fairlane died, my father purchased

an avocado-green Dodge that brought
my sisters and me to Southern California.

There is a Kodak shot of me in pajamas
in an Anaheim motel. It was minutes before

my father had arrived with our breakfast:
bagels and hard salami from a Jewish deli.

This is my palate's most lasting memory.
On our way to our first trip to Disneyland,

we saw no road kill on the highway,
no accidents where people died.

We had a flat tire, a problem my father
could not solve with his impeccable hands.

Then a state trooper appeared and showed
my father how to loosen the lug nuts first

before hoisting the car with the jack.
I remember his ineffectual hands,

the crowbar slipping constantly
from his sweaty palms. I can still see

the small gravel that lodged in them and how
he studied this surface of skin as if looking for answers.

FLASH ELORDE

It was in the city that had no autumns
where Flash Elorde landed a wacky left hook.

Harold Gomes's jaw popped like a dim lightbulb
and he stayed down a full seventy seconds after the bell.

This is a story of the old uncles from the valley of artichokes
who threw out their backs for fifteen cents an hour.

Summertime the old uncles flocked to the canneries,
then returned during the harvest months to cut artichokes,

the fragmented syntax of their stories yellow with age
like saved news clippings with a photo of a boxer

raised on the shoulders of men with slicked-back black hair
or a crew cut like their idol with a lightning bolt on his trunks.

For decades I believed that Flash Elorde had retreated
into Midwestern obsolescence to some armpit town

with two train silos and a quarry, where a misplaced old uncle
could be seen on the square, emerging from the pharmacy.

He'd be soft in the middle more like our local pharmacist
than like the aging but fit high-school coach

married to the church organist.
That was the fiction we spread to forget

the stories kindred with fish sauce and Del Monte
canned sardines, the old uncles yellowing like wallpaper

in downtown flophouses. But in 1956,
they put on their suits and laid down their cutting knives,

stood up from stooped labors to board a bus for San Francisco.
All true stories are autumnal. In 1956, on South Van Ness,

just beyond the crotch that split the Mission near Duboce,
Flash Elorde won six fights at the old Mission Gardens.

The year captured in the yellowing photograph
in a news clipping someone saved showing him caught

by the camera's lens in a sea of black hair,
arms raised in excess like summer gold.

THE BLOCK

Darrell's mother's red dress was chiffon
        and plunged at the neckline—a sleeveless job
that cupped her breasts with an *X*.
        I was on my way for a carton of milk
when she staggered out onto our street,

        the chiffon dress first, and then her mess—
her wig à la Diana Ross was off kilter,
        spider legs of mascara and blood
streaked down the shaft between her breasts.

        Saturday mornings she owned our street
when like the muezzin's call from his squat minaret
        she'd yell her boy's name clear as the nine strikes
of the bell from St. Agnes. I remember the long-stemmed rose
        my mother bent over when I gave her the first flower
I'd ever bought from the German florist in the Upper Haight.

        There are no long-stemmed roses
in this tundra, three-thousand-odd miles from my block.
        But there is a black cat named Snowball
and a stooped woman who walks him on a long leash,
        or winds the leash around the trunk of a sickly birch.

And Darrell is long gone like me.
        Blood on the sidewalk, and no shrubs, no gardens,
no tulips or rhododendrons, like at Sal's Famous
        Pizzeria where the man says,
"at Sal's there's no music, no music, no music."

Give me back my old block and morning hours
of cartoons before my chores, the cold glass of milk
        with the sourdough warming in the oven.
Let there be gardens in my bad old yard.

        Let all the flowers from the Upper Haight be
red dresses of chiffon with thorns drowned
        in beveled vases, the crown of one bending a little
with the blood-gorged petals of a rose.

And the circle was set in the sky
Like a pearl in a dark girl's palm.

—SAMUEL THE NAGID

THE IDEA OF NORTH

And what did you expect to see
      when you climbed up the stairs
to their bedroom only to discover
      your not-yet-old parents asleep
with the television on?

It has nothing to do with sadness
      when you wake and hear crows cawing
in the eerie trees, their gnarly branches
      like your unruly black hair in the wind.

The idea of north means to risk
      not coming back to what you've left behind,
to know the hour when the quiet window darkens,

      and the blue house disappears with the light.
You've learned to love the smooth bark of birches,
      the circle of trees outside. They must know
that you are nothing without them.

      You come back to that boy
standing in a room of two sleepers,
      their faces illuminated
by the television flicker; and what color

grief must be when you
      stand in the open,
vastly alone, blue August sky behind you.

PART 4

SUDDENLY OCTOBER

His wife had died of cancer.
There weren't enough details,
only this reason to wear a dark shirt.

In February, you would've found him,
hunchbacked, finishing nothing,
warming his hands over a meager fire.

Then in March,
pruning the vineyards. By September,
making wine.

In my dream, I see him as my autumnal
father with a gray fedora, doing his chores,
and then a big wind comes and steals away his hat.

The world is vast,
more boundless than all that birds inhabit.
It is a graspable earth where larks imply the sky,

entire cities of breaths and vistas.
Fugitive as watercolor,
the short walk to my maple trees dials light.

What is October but the smell of bonfire smoke,
when fathers leave and carry with them
their scent of mild decay.

RABBITS

Love's an immigrant. It works for almost nothing.
— LARRY LEVIS

Timothy hay mixes with the dirt we track,
trickles of tears from the milk carton,
and the kitchen air thickens with talk.

Mornings here are cold and colder.
We're starved and manic, amorous as nuns.
The woman is upset for not having slept.

Sees the pantry bare except for sugar and starch.
"We have love," the man says. Then brokers
an offer for their evening meal:

Tiger prawns with chili peppers and mint.
"Sounds swell," the woman says,
"Though you won't have time to cook it."

The man takes up the broom, hairy and fibrous.
He's rueful as a monk who sleeps in his coffin.
From where we feed, the radio calls for snow.

He casts his shadow, and names us
jackal and hay piranha, hogs of clover and grass.
Man-hours he wages on sweep and dust.

The woman sips her coffee,
regards the dust, the rasp of the broom,
the Nutrena pellets from the Polish store

where the immigrant breeder goes. She is now
at the mirror glossing her lips, combing her hair.
She's painted and dragged in corporate wool.

The man with two jobs is already late for one.
And for nothing he works for our insatiable bodies,
flat as pancakes, flattened by gorging.

Like an empty stomach the coffeemaker grumbles,
the radiators hiss. He showers and shaves,
joins Teddy Pendergrass on the air,

"Think I better let it go / looks like another love TKO."
And for our part, we understand the human.

ONE TRAIN

At Estación Abando in Bilbao,
daylight bathes the cramped sleeper car for two.
The couple slept in separate berths.
Don't look at them for too long,

because you might see yourself in their faces.
At this moment I am one of them,
about to be remanded to that place
between waiting and remembering.

A burst of broom lines the breakdown lane,
the big-breasted woman with a switch, trailed
by sleepwalking dogs, herds Holstein cows.
Memory tethers me to this earth.

I remember being twenty-six or twenty-seven
when the woman I had been seeing confessed
one day that she had been sleeping with someone else.
For some, truth is a serum of sweet sensation that floods

the body until it is reduced to a wisp of smoke.
For others, truth is the weight of oceans,
the sound of bridge cables snapping. My knees
weakened and whatever held me up buckled and released.

All I wanted to do was to lie down,
a spill of water on the ground.
Nothingness is the tactile testimonial of stars.
It is a voice in the graveyard shift,

a radio show of old songs. A desire to retrace
footsteps like children bent on turning back time.
I had drunk too much and wandered into a yard,
long with benches where children sit to eat

sandwiches from pails with a thermos of milk.
Above me, only hints of stars,
what the city lights allowed of the sky.
Every time I see you falling,

I get down on my knees and pray.
I didn't know it, but I was crowing
like dim birds in the night.
On my way, I ran into a woman
jumping out of a car. She was inconsolable.
Arms around her chest, tears on her face.
When she got closer, I held out
my pint of Jack Daniel's and said:

Maybe you could use this.
She looked at me up and down,
took the bottle from my hand,
then followed me to my apartment.

I was twenty-six or twenty-seven
when only things like this could happen.
I am sorry for telling you. But that's how it was.
She was pale and paler. There in the dark,

we were like an old couple going through the motions
of undressing and slipping into the covers.
She had small breasts, her butt round and firm,
her body a shadow of my own.

We didn't talk afterwards. She never gave me her name.
I remember a story about a man who gets off a train
and decides that this is the town
where he will live for the rest of his life.

All that remained from his past he kept inside a room
in which even the woman he married,
who loved him more than herself, never entered.
Lives entire companioned with people we hardly know.

If I could return to that night, I would change nothing.
Perhaps someone should tell the couple entering the new city
to endow the mystery that awaits them.
Go ahead, look at them as you see yourself holding on.

THE BEHEADING OF THE APOSTLE JAMES

But it was the head the executioner wanted.
>The head deposited in the basket as proof of service.

In Zurbarán's painting a dog appears
>in the lower left corner of the canvas; eye level

with the apostle contemplating the blade.
>In another gallery, a long rectangular canvas

depicts an interrogation. Four Middle Eastern men
>blindfolded. Behind their lips they are saying,

I will forget everything, forget even my name.
>The painter records what lapses into buried memory.

Thieves round the campfires in Zurbarán's day
>recount in rhyme the story of a dog that absconded

with the hand that didn't land in the basket.
>Prior to the miraculous boat that transported

his body to Galicia, a story of the apostle's
>left hand fueled a conference among thieves

the same hand blocked the blade
>as a visor would shield the sun.

James's mother, a simple woman,
>expected a high position for her son:

lording from a throne in the town square.
        There is an alternate cult

surrounding the knucklebone of a saint.
        The officers of corpses

are a driven bunch. They are my field marshals
        of doubt roaming the brush like a rumor of fire.

Once a finger of stars pointed to a field
        where the hermit Pelayo slept. And here

they've come with sunburnt faces,
        strangers to each with postcards in their hands.

MY BAD UNCLE

I saw him that night, his hands braceleted
behind his back—our neighborhood lit
like a bad uncle on a pint of scotch.

We all knew his sunnier days,
the perennial garden of his heart,
the shiny coins he doled out on his visits—.

How he'd sacrifice himself to woman whims:
his mother's, sisters', wife's, and lovers'. His gold Ford
Falcon that shuttled us back and forth to airports,

he was always available whenever we'd call.
He was a prince of the two-dollar cigar variety,
a happy man in love.

But goodness is mostly work and hardly pays a thing
to the soul when it has to eat alone.
His own goodness would tell him to drive

all day to his fake errands, or circle round
and around in the El with a hideaway bag
taking swigs between stops.

So one day when we weren't thinking,
or were thinking only of ourselves,
he parked outside a Denny's with his pistol

stuffed in his fanny pack. It was just a last-minute thing,
a quick bite then back to our house to sleep.
Takes very little to rouse the animal crouched in the garden:

The smirk of the local girl at the menu stand,
or the two boys spilling their Cokes on his new adidas.
A loud metal voice he seldom hears wells up

and he's shoving the snout of his pistol at someone's face.
Then two hours from Denny's, what another would term
a momentary lapse, the sirens and the cherry lights in our cul-de-sac.

Later in life I'd know what's in the doctor's cocktail,
potion in tablet form for the heart's slow undoing.
Only now there is a story my mother tells

of a sunny day in August when my bad uncle
drove us all to the beach in a golden car.
How we'd dry our wet suits on its regal hood,

we, newly arrived and eager for something
large yet undecided, our chins wet with strawberries,
and he, radiant in the whiskey-colored light.

BLUE SKY WITH THIEVES

Behind a gray civilian building
a boy with a gold tooth stood
unwrapping his Almond Joy.
Around him music blared from a box,
a tattooed man with a German shepherd.
And the sky, in its unfinished business,
kept bluing in the afternoon.

The waves of passersby swelled
and dissipated as we plundered
racks of polyester bell-bottoms
on the fourth floor of the Emporium.
Amid dim offices and department stores,
a ruined choir of car horns and fuel exhaust,
Miguel's imperial smile signaled
the rest of us to follow.

One afternoon he came to see me,
long after shoplifting had lost its urgency
in less dramatic fashion than the coastal faults.
And I, abandoned in my well of sleep,

on the hallway sofa when Miguel, all grown
in a shirt and pants I was certain he had purchased,
loomed over me like an extinct bird.
Miguel lived in the faraway alley of Natoma
deep in the South of Market, where our people,
despite the borders of industry, refuse extinction.

In 1663, Luca Giordano's painting of St. Michael
modeled the feathered hair that was the fashion of our day,
our hair groomed with a brush stuffed in our hip pockets.
In another time, we hung on scaffolds
for all in the passing carts to see: petty thieves
with eyes plucked out by crows.

It was in spring, not long after Watergate had blown,
that we exchanged small facts about each other
right there on the terra-cotta porch of my house.
The two of us so ordinary and dull, we had to force a laugh
like matrons amused by some endearing moment.

Once Miguel handed a dog a bite of Almond Joy,
its owner flipped and cursed us in his thick accent.
His arms coiled with ink, a twisted head of a snake,
and his dog's red tongue hanging. The tattooed man
heaved a buck knife at our boy.
Miguel bobbed and weaved to the music of our laughter.
He looped his wide belt around one hand,
the square silver buckle he swung heavy in the air.

We were a pair of dullards
with just enough sense between us
to look ahead at nothing.
Only sadness left after a good laugh
like this sky which tires from too much seeing.

HONOR LOAM

No rain in sight,
just this notion of flourish.
I am building an ark driven by voices.

I sink my nails and fingers in the dirt,
plant this package of marl, brine,
coffee grounds, and egg shells,

my peace offering
to the first lieutenant of worms
beneath this hairy soil.

I am thinking
about Pacifico Severino, the saint
who took no more than bread, soup, and water,

wore a hair shirt made of iron.
So much beauty in this garden that I grow
distrustful of all its mystery and trouble.

And saints I distrust as well—
the otherworldly statutes they abide by.
Holiness by earthly standards is slight madness.

There are days when silence floods over me
the way early May's heat reports the death of lilacs.
Today I honor loam, the birds and lilacs still in bloom.

In *The Conference of the Birds,*
the poet Attar says the soul is the body of desire,
and King Solomon spoke the language of birds.

I will forget what is immediate
like my father who tells me
the same story as if for the first time.

I will forget and maybe I will be spared.
I have this address, this house,
and everything that proves my existence,

                    this soil in my fingernails,
this human business of finding love.
If the soul is the body of desire,

then it must be transient,
a family living in their car, traveling people
with no fixed address or home.

NOTES

Quote in dedication page is from "Sea Poems" by Judah Halevi, a twelfth-century Jewish poet from Andalucía. Cited in María Rosa Menocal's *The Ornament of the World: How Muslims, Jews, and Christians Created a Culture of Tolerance in Medieval Spain*.

Mahsati Ganjavi is a twelfth-century Azery poet. She is best known for her love poems, but she underwent persecution for her brave poems condemning religious fanaticism.

"Boabdil's Eviction": Boabdil was also known as Muhammad XI, the last of the Nasrid rulers to occupy the Alhambra in Granada before capitulating to the Spanish monarchs in 1492.

"I want nothing else, only a hand…" comes from "Qasida of the Impossible Hand," a poem by Federico García Lorca (translated by Catherine Brown).

"Aubade": The poem's last line pays homage to César Vallejo's poem "Our Daily Bread" (translated by James Wright). The last line in Vallejo's poem is "here, in the oven of my heart…!"

In "One Train," the italicized lines come from the song "Bizarre Love Triangle" recorded by New Order (Warner/Chappell).

Ibn Nagrila or Samuel the Nagid is an 11th-century poet from Andalucía. Cited in María Rosa Menocal's *The Ornament of the World: How Muslims, Jews, and Christians Created a Culture of Tolerance in Medieval Spain*.

ACKNOWLEDGMENTS

Grateful acknowledgment is made to the editors and publishers of the following journals and anthology in which some of the poems in this collection were first published, sometimes in different versions.

Bat City Review: "Bilbao, Spain"
Bellevue Literary Review: "Flash Elorde"
Blue Mesa Review: "Song in the Form of a White Suit"
Clackamas Literary Review: "Allegra with Spirit"
The Gettysburg Review: "Mojácar" and "Rabbits"
Luna: "El Ave Christina" and "My Bad Uncle"
Many Mountains Moving: "Hoodlum Birds"
The North American Review: "The Factory"
Ploughshares: "The Law"
Poetry International: "Martyrdom of St. Eulalia"
Prairie Schooner: "Boabdil's Eviction," "Suddenly October," and "The Block" (as "Darrell")
Shenandoah: "Aubade"

"Aubade" also appears in *The Pushcart Prize XXVIII: Best of the Small Presses* (2004)

Thanks also to DePauw University for the John and Janice Fisher Fellowship and Amy M. Braddock Grants and to the Millay Colony for the Arts, Mary Anderson Center for the Arts, Virginia Center for the Creative Arts, Djerassi Resident Artists Program, the MacDowell Colony, Fundación Valparaíso, and Fondation Ledig-Rowohlt, Château de Lavigny for the space and time that allowed me to work on these poems. I am grateful to my wife, Karen, and friends Robert Wrigley, Eric Gamalinda, Derick Burleson, Oliver de la Paz, and Andrea Sununu for their careful attention and useful comments. I also want to extend my special thanks to my editor, Paul Slovak, and book designer, Sabrina Bowers.

Eugene Gloria was born in Manila, Philippines, and raised in San Francisco, California. His first book, *Drivers at the Short-Time Motel* (Penguin, 2000), was selected for the 1999 National Poetry Series and also received the Asian American Literary Award. He teaches at DePauw University and lives with his wife, Karen, in Greencastle, Indiana.

PENGUIN POETS

TED BERRIGAN
The Sonnets

JIM CARROLL
Fear of Dreaming:
*   The Selected Poems*
Living at the Movies
Void of Course

ALISON HAWTHORNE
   DEMING
Genius Loci

CARL DENNIS
New and Selected Poems
*   1974–2004*
Practical Gods
Ranking the Wishes

DIANE DI PRIMA
Loba

STUART DISCHELL
Dig Safe

STEPHEN DOBYNS
Mystery, So Long
Velocities: New and
*   Selected Poems:*
*   1966–1992*

AMY GERSTLER
Crown of Weeds
Ghost Girl
Nerve Storm

EUGENE GLORIA
Drivers at the Short-Time
*   Motel*
Hoodlum Birds

DEBORA GREGER
Desert Fathers, Uranium
*   Daughters*
God
Western Art

TERRANCE HAYES
Hip Logic
Wind in a Box

ROBERT HUNTER
Sentinel and Other Poems

MARY KARR
Viper Rum

JACK KEROUAC
Book of Blues
Book of Haikus
Book of Sketches

ANN LAUTERBACH
Hum
If in Time: Selected
*   Poems, 1975–2000*
On a Stair

CORINNE LEE
PYX

PHYLLIS LEVIN
Mercury

WILLIAM LOGAN
Macbeth in Venice
Night Battle
The Whispering Gallery

MICHAEL MCCLURE
Huge Dreams:
*   San Francisco and Beat*
*   Poems*

DAVID MELTZER
David's Copy: The
*   Selected Poems of*
*   David Meltzer*

CAROL MUSKE
An Octave Above
*   Thunder*
Red Trousseau

ALICE NOTLEY
The Descent of Alette
Disobedience
Mysteries of Small Houses

PATTIANN ROGERS
Generations

STEPHANIE STRICKLAND
V: WaveSon.nets/Losing
*   L'una*

ANNE WALDMAN
Kill or Cure
Marriage: A Sentence
Structure of the World
*   Compared to a Bubble*

JAMES WELCH
Riding the Earthboy 40

PHILIP WHALEN
Overtime: Selected Poems

ROBERT WRIGLEY
Lives of the Animals
Reign of Snakes

MARK YAKICH
Unrelated Individuals
*   Forming a Group*
*   Waiting to Cross*

JOHN YAU
Borrowed Love Poems